WATER FORCE

The power of learning to swim

Contents

So, I rang up my local swimming bath, and I said, "Is this the local swimming bath?" He said, "It depends on where you're calling from."

— Tim Vine

Introduction

There was a swimming pool at my primary school. We were given regular lessons, but they didn't seem to make much difference. And once I had a swimming birthday party for which my mother made a swimming pool cake, à la Jane Asher. You might find that very cake if you dig in the archives.

Of the swimming lessons, I remember the others being able to do somersaults in the water and retrieve black rubber bricks from the bottom of the pool. Attempting either sent gallons of water gushing up my nose so became out of the question. The other thing was, while all my classmates would glide back and forth, up and down the pool, I was able only to bring up the rear at the most excruciatingly slow pace, splashing along in doggy paddle. I never considered myself unable to swim because I ended up surviving every swimming session without the help of a lifeguard, but I was not a swimmer in the functional sense.

You needn't worry, I was good at other things. I could make people laugh. I could memorise and recite poetry from the age of two, making my family think I was a child prodigy. I could also juggle, ride horses, ski moguls, cycle with no hands and memorise every song, musical, film and conversation I ever heard, saw or had. I had some early success riding horses and as a junior show jumper even ended up on the Great Britain Under 18 squad for a season. So my inability to swim really was not grounds for concern.

Showjumping became my first great addiction. And it wasn't without water. My horse, Rocky, threw me off in the water jump at Forest Edge, a show centre in Norfolk – Rocky had a charming sense of humour. The worst thing about falling into the Forest Edge water jump was the black, grooved rubber matting. Maybe it was designed to cushion the blow? It left black stripes on my skin-tight white breeches and the water seemed to help set the stain.

It's thanks to various successes in the showjumping arena that I developed a taste for prizes. Mainly money and rosettes, and sometimes trophies, cups, shields, sashes and medals. It was these prizes that I realised I missed when I had a not-quite-mid-life yen to return to showjumping.

Instead of a lifestyle upheaval, I took up running, simply to get the medals and to scratch the itch. I sought always to maximise the outcome of my effort, for example, if I had two 10k events in a month, I'd enter an online mileage challenge to get more medals overall. Like any addiction, I needed a bigger dose to get the same hit, so I entered the London Marathon thinking that this might be my route to the best finisher's medal around. And I was probably right until a bit of research revealed the London Classics challenge which tempted me with a truly excellent-looking medal and continued in the spirit of maximising outcome (four medals for the effort of three).

If I wanted it – which I already did – I'd have to diversify to include cycling and swimming. Cycling? No problem (Remember the aforementioned ability to ride a bike with no hands?)! And… swimming. Not just any swimming either. For this particular challenge, I would have to swim two miles round the Serpentine, Hyde Park.

By now I had the medal in my crosshairs. I'd locked onto it the way that terriers lock onto their rodent prey.

I trained for and ran the London Marathon in October 2021, slightly later in the year than the traditional April date because of the pandemic upheaval. My entry was confirmed for the one hundred mile Ride London bike ride, in May 2023 and also for the two-mile swim in September 2022.

By April 2022 I had a super-looking swimming costume that I'd agonised over buying. It was black with strategic white piping, which I thought would be flattering. And maybe it was, but it didn't make me want to try it out. I made a few attempts to go to the pool. I even got there and parked, but instead of swimming, I ended up going for a run around the area of the swimming pool and avoided setting foot inside the building. I did some stretching before and after every run near the door of the building. From there I could smell the pool and I couldn't stand it. And that was my starting point – an aversion to the very smell of swimming.

HARRIET GOULD

Chapter 1
The Beginning

The Saxon Leisure Centre pool is the closest public pool to my house. Run by Central Bedfordshire Council, the description on the website explains their mission is "... for everyone in the local community to be active for at least 30 minutes, 5 times a week..." A noble mission. And one I'd have to exceed by far if I wanted to achieve my goal. My goal was to complete the annual two-mile swim event in the Serpentine in Hyde Park as part of the London Classics challenge. Swimming in the Serpentine might not seem normal, but it is. Since 1846, the Serpentine Swimming Club has organised an annual 100-yard race on Christmas Day. Then, in 1903, according to the Serpentine Swimming Club, the author, J.M. Barrie used the occasion to promote the stage debut of his play, Peter Pan, by donating the Peter Pan Cup to be presented to the winner in perpetuity. The lake itself was conceived by the wife of King George IV, Queen Caroline, in 1730. The landscaping was implemented by then Royal gardener, Charles Bridgeman, in what must have seemed an ambitious redevelopment project at the time. It included damming the River Westbourne and joining up the smaller ponds in the park to make the lake.

When I arrived at my local Council pool, psyched for my inaugural swim, the woman at the desk shook her head apologetically and told me the pool was "closed for the kiddies", to "come back in three hours" and would I "like a timetable"? In my life as a swimmer, swimming timetables feature only twice. In both cases they are works of anti-art; grids and grids covered in dots and tiny writing. I de-psyched myself, learnt the dreadful timetable dot system and three hours later I was contorting myself into my smart new costume. I never got into the habit of putting my costume on under my clothes and whenever I did, I forgot to take underwear for afterwards.

Approaching the pool, I took it all in. The distracting echo and the bright blueness of the pool contrasted with the hazily dark lighting around one (whole) half of the area, which included a baby pool. I hoped, as I climbed down the ladder into the shallow end, that I'd miraculously be able to swim, just because I wanted to. Unfortunately, even getting into the pool was more of a challenge than I'd expected. What if I went in too fast? What if it was too cold? What if a wave engulfed me and I drowned? (There were no waves). Bracing myself for all of the above, I got in without incident. I'd never been any good at dealing with contrasting temperatures, especially warm to cold. It was an ok 29C. Half the pool was segmented into lanes, and powerful junior swimmers, who looked as though they were in training for the Olympics, were performing a relay. They were zooming up the 25-metre pool with the next swimmer diving in over the previous swimmer's head. I studied them intently, then tried to swim, still with the mindset that if I wanted to do it enough, I would be able to, instantly.

One terrifying moment later, I had disproved my theory. Gasping and spluttering, I heaved my head back and planted my feet on the bottom of the pool. I must have nearly drowned. Half the pool went up my nose, the other half down my throat and my eyes felt as if they were bleeding. "My God", I thought. "How am I ever going to figure this out?" I decided to paddle for a while before trying again. It was no good. Even putting my face flat on the water made me feel as though I was going to die. Thinking it through, I looked around for some help. Flapping and splashing with my head as far out of the water as it could be, I doggy-paddled to the side to catch the attention of the lifeguard. She tried to explain to me how to breathe for a front crawl. It sounded complicated since my immediate problem wasn't how to breathe but how to stop the water from flooding my face. She made the eminently sensible suggestion of booking a lesson. Of course, I wanted the lesson there and then, which wasn't an option, so I got out and went home to worry about it instead.

I felt so discouraged that under normal circumstances I might have never swum again. But my hand was being forced. Or I was forcing my hand. To reinforce my commitment to my mission, I decided that I'd take the advice given to me by many people which was to note my progress in a diary. I hoped it'd help me make some! The next day, I went to Lillywhites, the sports department store that's taken up one corner of Piccadilly Circus since 1925. I looked up the history of the shop and sadly there's no reference to swimming. There is a tragic link to water though. In 1930, the Lillywhite family supplied a flying kit to the pilot, Amy Johnson, long-distance record-setter who famously crashed to her death in the Thames Estuary in 1941. There had been an attempt to save her, but that only resulted in the death of the Lieutenant Commander, Walter Fletcher, who captained the vessel that had rushed to her rescue. Fletcher had ended up jumping into the freezing water when initial rescue efforts had failed. He died days later in hospital from exposure.

Taking the stairs, I made my way to the swimming section on the top floor. One other customer was browsing in the eaves and no one else was. I wished I hadn't, but I asked his advice. "You can get infections from lakes," he warned, "so don't let any water in under any circumstances." That'll teach me to ask for advice when all I wanted was reassurance. I chose and paid for goggles and earplugs and walked back down the stairs feeling fairly uneasy. Lake bacteria hadn't crossed my mind before.

It was already May and not even early May. It was 12 May 2022, four months from the date of the swim, and I was even less able to swim than I had been before I began to try. Luckily, my friend-cum-personal trainer, Juliet, had noted the tight deadline and taken control of the situation. Juliet Clarke is known professionally as PTJoolz and known among friends as Joolz. She is the perfect personal trainer and anyone would be lucky to be under her tutelage. Joolz booked us both in for a swimming lesson rather than sending me off to face the music on my own. This is a typical example of her on-tap kindness, and it left me conflicted because I was grateful and terrified in equal measure.

The evil hour arrived. Joolz picked me up and drove us up the road to nearby Tadlow. We arrived at a somewhat Mediterranean-style house. The garden had spiky plants in terracotta pots. The pool was concealed inside another building that wouldn't have looked out of place on the Costa del Sol and seemed at odds with the English countryside. It's easy enough to build a swimming pool in the garden, as proven by @alexdodman on TikTok. You don't even need any experience, as he mentions now and then.

Out popped lovely, smiley teacher Heather, from the pool house. She was wearing a black swimming outfit, which had long shorts and half sleeves. After the usual introductions, I quickly blurted out that I was scared of the water going up my nose. Heather had an immediate solution. She suggested I wear a nose clip - another terrifying notion – how would I breathe at all?! The pool was short – only four or five metres long – and so many million factors less intimidating than the local Council pool. Plus, it was as warm as a bath.

With encouragement from Heather, I put my goggled, nose-clipped face in the water, only to face yet another horror. Relieved of the distracting trauma of water going up my nose, I was now free to notice the sight of the pool below the waterline. It was panic-inducing. I'd seen below waterlines before. I'd been snorkelling before, in the shallows of the Cayman Islands where I met turtles the size of beds for medium-sized dogs, starfish brighter than the sun and puppy-like shoals of stingray; but the sight of the bottom of this little pool seemed menacing. Maybe it was the lack of sea life?

The blueness seemed bigger than it had from above the water which was a bigger shock compared to how un-intimidating the pool had initially seemed. Had I accidentally got cocky in that short time? The terrible trouble was the physical effect it had on me. I panicked and stood up, gasping. Heather, clearly used to handling every possible variable from her students, slid into the pool to perform an obviously well-used "calm down" routine. "Breathe. That's it. No rush." But there was a rush and by now, all three of us were slightly wondering how I was going to manage to learn to swim in time.

I kicked myself for not starting earlier in the year. February perhaps. Or even March! Imagine entering a swimming event before knowing how to swim. I had until 17 September 2022 to learn how to swim two miles in a lake with hundreds of other people. In a 25-metre pool, two miles equates to 120 lengths or so. And here, today, I couldn't even manage to look around under the water, let alone anything else. After forty-five minutes of practice dunks and face-down drills, I gradually became able to try a bit of swimming at the same time as being scared of the sight of the pool. What a relief. Throughout, I tried my best to impersonate what I thought a professional swimmer might look like, and by the end of the lesson I had a breaststroke mantra and a front crawl mantra. I wasn't planning to use breaststroke for the event, but Heather convinced me I should learn and train with both and I wasn't really in a position to object. Just before we left, Heather gave me a swimming hat with Tadlow Swimming School branding on it, and she gave Joolz a warning not to enter the swim. "I know her type" she said, nodding in my direction, "she'll end up being fast and leave everyone behind". I felt slightly encouraged by her words.

Next time in the pool, I managed to remember everything Heather had taught me. I had even felt keen to get there to try it out. I swam away from the shallow end, with my face down in the water. The only difference here was that the floor fell away about halfway along. The mass of water increased to form what must have qualified as a "body" of water and the sight of flailing legs randomly jabbing at the surface took me by surprise. I had to stop in a panic, but it was OK, this time I knew what to do. First, do a bit of "calm-down" breathing, then get on with it. Be scared and do it anyway without panicking.

The funny thing is that I'm sure there have been several times when I have thought that I couldn't see a way of doing something and subsequently not done it. I kept telling myself, this was it. I was committed, there was a time limit and no way out. No way out. In reality, of course, there was a way out, but I felt as if there wasn't because I wanted the medal. Plus, I wanted the effort it had taken to run the marathon (mainly the months of training) to go to a greater purpose and I still thought the bike ride would be easy, compared to the run and the swim. So there was no way out. I had to do it. At least I had my one lesson's worth of instruction to fall back on this time. Stay calm, face back in the water, and watch the flailing legs above and the endless depths below. Get on with it, turn your head to the side, take a tiny breath and carry on. When I signed up, I didn't think I considered the enormity of learning to do something from utter scratch. Maybe I wouldn't have signed up if I realised how un-fine I would turn out to be. I finished the length, somehow forcing myself to stay calm as I looked through the water.

While I caught my breath at the deep end, feet planted on the little safety ledge, a woman bobbed up and stopped with me. She'd swum the whole length on her side, with glasses instead of goggles and her wispy fair hair was bone dry. She smiled at me the way people do when they can see you're struggling. "The pool's lovely isn't it," she said. I explained that my frame of reference was limited. Before I could stop myself, I admitted how scared I was of the enormity of my task. "Oh, my dear," she said. "What are you scared of?!" "The depth! The dark! The distance! The people!... What's not to be scared of?" "No," she said. "You don't need to worry because you're in control and at any time you can stop and roll onto your back." She told me it was a tactic she'd used in Cyprus, where all the swimming pools are cold. I liked the sound of her idea. It reminded me of the advice Grandma Diana has always given me about work (though never actually taken!) "You should ring them up and tell them you're too tired to do any work". I tried another length, continuing to make myself look around under the water. I was still choking every three or four strokes, which slowed my already painfully slow pace.

The next time I stopped at the deep end, I joined a man who was having a rest. He was maybe in his late 60's. We had a brief chat and he told me he'd been prescribed swimming to get fit after having had a heart attack and that he'd missed swimming during the pandemic. Even more heart-rending than a heart attack, he told me how his daughter and his wife had caught Covid and died. I couldn't help but stay and listen to him. How he walked to the pool and smelled fish and chips on the way. What his daughter was like... Eventually, I tore myself away for another length. This length was far more calm than all the others. That man's story had injected some perspective. In my riding days, training young horses to be show jumpers, I always made sure that the horses finished their training on a good note. After that calm length, it felt like a good moment to transfer this technique, so I climbed out of the pool and went home.

Chapter 2
Next Steps

I've never believed in the saying, "You can't choose your family, but you can choose your friends." I don't think you can choose either. I can't think of a time when I have chosen a friend. How would I know who to choose or what to do about it? I have naturally occurring friends and, as luck would have it, three of the closest of them are better than average swimmers. One in particular, Jacqui, turned out to be a vital cog in my learn-to-swim team.

Jacqui Mackenzie Gray and I met in 2005 when I began working at a contract publishing company in Hatfield. I remember on my first day asking her what she 'did'. "I'm an actress" she'd said, "What do you do?". "I'm a show jumper". Funny how we assumed that we both did something other than the job we were ostensibly there to do. We got to work striking advertising deals for the various publications in our charge, from Crufts and Royal Ascot to National Boat Shows and Taste of London. By 2019, Jacqui had started her own business. Almost immediately, the pandemic battered her around the head, and she'd had to adapt in shape-shifting ways to keep the show on the road while the world was closed.

By the time I called her to wail about the huge and arguably pointless task I'd set myself, it seemed that the idea of having regular swimming dates appealed to her. "I'll help you!" she insisted, almost pleadingly down the phone. It was a huge relief to have her on my learn-to-swim team. On 11 June 2022, I used Jacqui's guest pass for the Nuffield Gym pool in St Albans. It isn't a glamorous place. Or even appealing in any way. The outside is industrial. All galvanised steel and fibreglass. It makes you think twice about going in. An acrid smell of sweat, deodorant and disinfectant greets you as you walk in. I have always had an aversion to gyms. The idea of indoor exercise always disgusted me. Hundreds of people, maybe more, sweating over everything and gulping the same air. If I had been on my own that day or if I hadn't had a deadline, I might have left immediately. The main pool there is 1.4 metres deep all the way along and the water is quite cool. I had my huge goggle and the nose clip, which was not comfortable, but it did at least mean one route to drowning was eliminated without much effort.

Jacqui turned out to be a sympathetic and hugely encouraging training partner, and between breezing up and down the pool a million times like a mermaid, she'd stop to say, "You'll be brilliant" and "You're made for swimming." My two or three strokes in a row felt so far from brilliant it's hard to describe, but it was nice to hear. I felt a little bit like an old tramp steamer with a leak, but at least there seemed to be progress. After swimming in this pool, you have the reward of a steam room and a choice of two saunas. There's even a smaller (warmer) pool which they use for aqua aerobics classes and other lessons.

You probably already know that every part of the front crawl arm stroke has a name and an optimum technique. The part of the stroke (in front crawl) where you draw your arm towards you is called the 'catch'. As I got more used to the water, I started noticing how hard I was finding it to draw my arm back for the catch and I couldn't make out why. How hard could it be to keep a straight arm throughout the stroke?! Eventually, I complained in frustration to Jacqui. And thank goodness I did! "Draw an 'S' with your arm" she explained. An 'S' was quite easy with my left arm, maybe being left-handed helped, but it took a while to get the hang of it with my right arm.

I went back to the St Albans pool two days later and discovered that I had left my goggles at home. There is a small selection of items for sale near the entrance, including a range of goggles. The goggles I chose were shiny and very impressive-looking compared to the clear uni-lense I'd been using. I felt instantly more water-literate and the tinted lenses softened the appearance of the bottom of the pool, making the bright blue seem less threatening. I'm sure these goggles contributed to my best length in the pool up to that point. I kept a good rhythm and felt as though I could have possibly carried on if the pool had been longer. The diary entry for this day doesn't exist because the feeling gave me a flashback to an occasion where a great achievement turned out less well. I worried that if I noted the progress down, it would spell failure in the future, so I noted this moment of progress in my head only.

Session 11 sticks in my mind as well as in my diary. It was the first time I had proper kit problems. You don't have to be a swimmer to know how infuriating it is when a piece of equipment fails to work as it should. If you are a swimmer, you'll have extra sympathy with the goggles and hat problems I suffered during this session. Paranoid about my hair drying out from all the chlorine, I had been slapping a bucket of conditioner on before swimming. On this occasion, it backfired. The conditioner had made it hard for the hat to grip my head, and it had somehow spread over the goggle straps too, making it impossible to move without the hat and goggles slipping off. Conditioner was also getting in my eyes, which stung to high heaven and put me in even more of a pickle.

It was so distracting. I kept breaking my rhythm and started choking on the water again. At the end of one very long length, I snapped. Chucking my hat across the pool, I yelled at Jacqui, demanding that she tell me why I still couldn't do it. She didn't rise. I waded over to my hat, snatched it up, and threw it again, glaring at Jacqui, staring hard at her as though she was purposely concealing the secret of swimming from me. Luckily for me, she still didn't rise. Instead, never dropping eye contact, she oh-so-calmly took a deep breath, indicating that I should do the same. Then she passed me my hat and said I was doing well. Quite saintly when you think about it. At moments like this, I was even more grateful than usual for having such good friends. I couldn't see the future. I had no real basis from which to tell myself 'It just takes time'. Two miles, choking on bacteria-laden lake water, not being able to put my feet down every 25 metres and travelling as slowly as could be was so unappealing that I had to recommit myself. Instead of learning to swim, which I suppose I had done after a fashion by this point, I committed to trying to up my game by spending more time in the pool, using water instead of conditioner to protect my hair and studying modern swimming techniques every time I looked at my phone.

So I started swimming three times a week and paid more attention to other resources at my disposal. For example, the many swimming accounts on Instagram. @skillsntalents was one of a few I found particularly helpful because they shared 3D biometric models of every swimming stroke. It is so much easier to watch the mechanics of the stroke broken down in this way, compared to trying to watch someone in real time in the pool. Little by little, bits of technique started to sink in.

Understanding the technique and the way each limb is supposed to move was helpful, to say the least. I felt if I could grasp that, I would stand a chance of improving. It reminded me of when you go to a dance exercise class. Until you know the steps, you keep moving in the wrong direction and crashing into people. If I could improve my technique, I hoped I'd be able to improve my so-called 'feel' of the water.

My new strategy was beginning to pay off, but during every subsequent swim in the pool, a small thought had started to grow. It was all very well swimming here, in the clear, clean pool but ultimately I wasn't going to be swimming in a pool; I would have to swim in a lake. I made the mistake of Googling "how deep is the Serpentine." Why did I do that? It said 5.3 metres. For a while, I decided to be pleased that I was getting comfortable in the pool. I made a pact with myself that at the next opportunity, I would swim in natural water.

HARRIET GOULD

Chapter 3
A Change of Scene

Shockingly, it was already the end of June 2022, and I had booked a few days in Málaga. My mother rents a flat there and encourages friends and family to make use of it whenever they can. This was the first time I'd taken up her kind offer, and I was meeting a friend there, Bjorn, who lives in Stockholm. Bjorn Blomkvist and I met in Liverpool in 2018, and both were involved in the EuCheMS congress. We were at the same table at the semi-formal dinner which was called the Congress Banquet. Surely anything with such a name can only be an anti-climax. Not so in this case. Liverpool Anglican Cathedral (not to be confused with Liverpool Metropolitan Cathedral) was dressed for the occasion. Her west window with its neon sign by Tracey Emin was just one of many extraordinary features. A wonderful setting for the start of an enduring if long-distance friendship. My only stipulation for our few days in Málaga was that I wanted to swim in the sea. I had never swum properly in the sea. It was always more of a restful – or playful – experience than an activity. And I usually didn't go in if there were waves. Even small ones. Apart from one time in Sri Lanka. A group of us were on a beach in Marissa – just along the south coast of the island, near the quite famous "Turtle Bay." The coastline goes in and out, and the bits that go out are mountainous, so the view from the beach includes bulging forests that dip down into the sea, big rocks that look like outlandish beings and waves that come in rhythmically as if there were a wave machine helping them to keep in time. Seduced by the magic, I had decided I wanted to learn to surf. But it turns out you can't surf if you can't swim. I spent an afternoon learning how to dive waves which is also quite hard if you can't swim and is another prerequisite for surfing. It was mostly OK if I held my nose, but the waves were vast and when I misjudged them I was tumbled back to the beach, as though I were a rag doll in a washing machine.

The sea in Málaga is less "surfy" than the sea in Sri Lanka, so at least I didn't have any massive waves to judge or misjudge. Every day I swam a little bit and was almost shocked by how manageable I was finding it. There was one day I got a bit carried away – by a current. But, without hesitating, as the sweet woman in the Council pool had suggested, I turned on my back and swam myself within range of the beach. It was a little bit harder to work out when to breathe while out at sea because of the way the water moved, but otherwise, it was a triumph. A triumph I relived a hundred times to poor Bjorn.

Just as I got home, a chance trip to Italy came up. It's a little bit convoluted. Leigh Jeffs and I met via a mutual conference called Science and The Parliament. On this occasion, he told me all about this wonderful place he was visiting with friends. I felt quite envious and said to him "I'm so jealous! I wish I could come!" "Well, you must come then!" he exclaimed. We were staying in a seventeenth century, slightly down-at-heel house in Erbusco, Lombardy. I looked it up and learned that this beautiful area is a place where, since medieval times, people have cultivated vineyards, olive groves and vegetable gardens. If you go there, look out for Franciacorta's sparkling wines, because they've won awards for their quality and geographical authenticity from the Denomination of Controlled and Guaranteed Origin, according to Wikipedia.

The house itself was not wildly attractive from the outside, but it did have a 15-metre pool in the garden and was conveniently located between Lake Garda and Lake Iseo. There were loads of ancient pictures and family memorabilia everywhere. I worked from the study, which was very splendid and filled with dark wooden furniture, including crammed bookshelves, huge portraits and a big wooden globe on a stand. It was cool and smelled musty, almost nice, but not quite. The kitchen, when all of us were there, was the best part. Vast sinks, endless pots, pans, bowls and jugs. No shortage of space or utensils. We cooked and prepped masses of food — including fresh figs which were abundant — and I got to know my hosts. Emma greeted me with a huge hug. Her partner Julian — as vibrant as a jester — drew portraits of us in crayon while we sunbathed.

For some reason, I felt self-conscious about swimming properly in the pool. Was it the contrast between holiday mode and swimming hat, goggles and nose clip mode? Who knows. The second morning, I dared to venture down before breakfast to swim some lengths. I'd had a trial dip the day before, so getting in was fine. The water in this pool seemed more salty than chlorinated. Lighter or thinner somehow. I started my lengths, setting a target of ten. I'm not sure if I managed ten because I'm terrible at keeping count. There are so many other things to think about between the beginning and end of each length. The lining of the pool was much lighter blue than other pools I'd been in. There were no lines for guidance and the sight of the floor dropping away did what it always does to me, but I gritted my teeth and got on with it, pushing through the fear. Despite this success story, I didn't swim any more lengths during the holiday. I was reading John Mortimer's *Summer's Lease* on my Kindle and that, more than anything else, put me off getting back in the pool. I watched the others playing on the diving board and shuddered at the thought of joining in.

I did, however, manage a small swim in Lake Garda. It was more of a paddle than a swim. Getting in was the first hurdle. We found a perfect place; a concrete platform where syrup-skinned people were bathing in the sun. We had to climb down the rocks at the side of the platform to get to the 'beach'. The lake was the brightest blue green. It looked refreshing and clean. Close up, it was crystal clear and quite choppy because of all the boats whizzing everywhere. I carefully picked my way into the water across the rocks and stones. It was impossible to go quickly. I only went in far enough to be able to float comfortably without bumping into a rock.

I felt almost ecstatic afterwards. Fully cooled and marvelling at yet another swimming first.

Chapter 4
Home But Not Dry

Back in the homeland, the St Albans pool felt like an old friend. Pretty quickly… that niggling thought crept back in. I needed to swim in a lake. Properly. I hadn't put my face in Lake Garda because I hadn't been wearing goggles. I didn't think I'd get away with two miles of swimming in the Serpentine with my head above water. And I didn't want to anyway. I wanted to do it as properly as I could manage. To me, that meant the face had to go in the water. So I set about making enquiries. A quick search told me that Milton Country Park had the best lake for learning to swim in natural water, so I called them. A woman answered the phone and informed me, "They had the blue-green algae", so there'd be no swimming in the lake. I don't know how much you know about this phenomenon of nature, and I'm far from an expert, but I can tell you that blue-green algae is a naturally occurring spore that forms on water in hot weather and if the "levels are high" it can be harmful to humans. I shuddered at the thought of it. Yet another hazard to come to terms with. Swimming, it had turned out, was so far beyond the technical for me. It challenged almost every fear I had. You know when you run, never mind how far, there's not much to be scared of. And it's roughly the same when you cycle, perhaps apart from the cost of the kit. But swimming was testing the outer limits of my belief in myself. Reeling from the news of the blue-green algae, I managed to listen just closely enough to note down the name of an open-water swimming instructor who would find an alternative lake to teach me in. An open-water swimming instructor! Just what I needed. Why hadn't I thought of that? Perhaps because, in addition to being scared of everything to do with swimming, I also knew nothing about swimming. Not a thing.

When I rang to explain my predicament, Val was enthusiastic in the way instructors of any physical pursuit tend to be. I'm not sure if it's the prospect of new business or the excitement of a person showing interest in the thing that they are passionate about. Maybe both? So we set a date. We would meet at Paxton Pits lake at the crack of dawn on Saturday, 20 August 2022, for what would be my first proper lake swim.

The lake itself was well hidden down endless bumpy tracks. The signs were hand-made and misleading. I turned left at a huge rack of old paddle boards and aimed at the neat line of parked cars. This, by the way, was the first time I was going to have the chance to use the wetsuit I'd had in my possession for more than six months. My first attempt to use it was in January at a beach in Norfolk. I'd ended up not going in because the sea looked like a brown, heaving monster and no other people were swimming or even attempting to swim. I doubt I'd go in now if it looked like that, despite my advancing abilities and ever-growing bravery.

I parked the car in line with the others and took in what I could see. Beyond the hedgerow was a sweep of lawn down to the edge of the lake where plenty of familiar-looking lake plants sprouted. On the left was a grubby white Portakabin with a big, square veranda. Wetsuits were drip-drying over the balustrades. Beyond the cabin was a shipping container which, it turned out, had been converted into changing rooms with showers and loos.

I pulled my wetsuit half on and crossed the lawn to meet instructor Val. She made me read some safety things and sign a disclaimer. Val was incredibly kind and asked lots of questions about the swimming I'd done and debated extra bits of kit with me, for example, little neoprene socks. Her argument for wearing them was they'd make my feet marginally bigger, "like flippers", which would mean I'd go faster. I wasn't keen on sourcing a pair of my own, so it didn't make sense to wear the pair she offered.

At the water's edge, there was a carpet of astroturf laid out to stop the way into the lake getting churned up like the gateway of a horse's paddock. Val led the way, walking backwards and stopping every few steps. "Just stop here and feel the ground under your feet". I obeyed, thinking carefully about how squashy the astroturf felt. As we went in further, the water began to seep through the wetsuit. I thought it'd be colder than it was. You're probably used to wearing a wetsuit but remember this was my first time and I found it hard to tell whether I was wet. Now in the water, up to our waists. Val was swirling her hands around. "Now we touch the water," she said. I touched the water, imitating her actions. It felt similar to all other water I had felt. "And now we smell the water", cupping her hands together, she scooped the water up and sniffed it. As though hypnotised, I copied her. The Paxton Pits lake water smelled of all the best mornings rolled into one. The whole earth with moss on the side. It was comforting in a way.

After the sensory initiation, we paddled in a bit further and began to tread water. It was actually quite nice not being restricted, as I suddenly saw it, by the floor of the pool. Then it was time to do the thing I was most apprehensive about, which was swimming with my face in the water. I checked that the nose clip was in place and went for it. The water was dark but clear. I could see plenty of weeds, but they were dotted here and there, as though someone had thought about it in a landscaping sense. Most of the weeds seemed to be Egeria. I don't know about weeds, but the online description of Egeria is a match with what was down there. I couldn't see the actual bottom of the lake; what was visible simply faded away into darkness. After a few stints of 10 strokes or so, we stopped to tread more water and discuss matters. It seemed remarkable to me that I hadn't had a panic attack. Not that I'm prone to them per se, it just seemed like a possibility, given the trepidation I felt about swimming in a lake.

Slightly too soon, Val nudged me off my self-congratulatory perch by asking "why do you wear the nose clip?" I wasn't ready for this. I explained hurriedly to Val that I used the nose clip to prevent early death by water inhalation. The moment I had been dreading arrived. "I think you should try without the nose clip" Val said, clearly not understanding the huge impact it was having on me. I don't know how to convey this effectively with as much power as it deserves; but when I am under official instruction I cannot not do what I am told. In some ways it's useful, because it means I'm able to precisely convert instruction into action. I have always been able to. In other ways it's a bind because I have to do things I don't want to do or that I feel unready to do. My various coaches in the horsey years found it a blessing. PT Joolz always seems thrilled by it too... "You always do exactly what I say" to which I always reply, "what else am I supposed to do?" Out in the lake that day, I had no choice but to whip the nose clip off, wedge it to my watch strap and take some instructions about how not to die without a nose clip.

"Bubble, bubble, bubble," was the instruction. I was being instructed to blow bubbles with my nose. Was that all? Blowing bubbles was the difference between life and death?! Then the real revelation came. "You probably weren't nearly dying, you just might have thought you were". It had felt as though I was! So off we went again, blowing bubbles all the way. And all of a sudden I felt free! It was as if I was part of the water rather than being a foreign object in the water. We'd made it about two thirds of the way around the lake and the bubble-blowing and intermittent weed-sightings made me feel like an intrepid explorer. An intrepid amphibious explorer. It was a relief to have tried a lake and survived. We'd swum for about an hour – it was the longest I'd swum without touching the floor. I couldn't stand up properly when I got out, I was desperate for the loo and kept toppling to the side while trying to get my feet in my flip-flops. It was infuriating. "What's wrong with my legs?"

During the post-swim "wash-up," sitting at a picnic table, I ate a glorious bacon sandwich and Val predicted I would certainly be able to swim the two miles. I was glad she thought so, but questioned her conviction, as two miles was quite a long way, especially considering that I was still such a novice. Val assured me that she'd thought I was a swimmer from the moment she'd seen me walk across the lawn. I felt suitably reassured, and I was ecstatic to have graduated from the nose clip!

HARRIET GOULD

Chapter 5
Grandma Diana

After swimming, I visited Grandma Diana – a formerly formidable swimmer; she swam for Cheltenham and played water polo in her youth. That afternoon, I told her that I was learning to swim. She said it was her favourite thing and her best sport. I asked her whether she'd like to swim now. She replied "you must be joking. I'm not swimming now" Grandma Diana's 'now' is a reference to her advancing years. She is 90 now, and I'm only sorry I can't write her intonation or accent in text. You wouldn't believe me anyway. You have to hear her to know I'm not exaggerating.

When I told Grandma Diana about swimming in the lake, she changed her tune. "What? The lake? I shouldn't go in a lake if I were you. It's dangerous. You should stay in the swimming pool where people can keep an eye on you". Her tone had grown grave, and she had a pained expression on her face. Almost jumpy, she turned to Uncle Jeremy and, waving her arm in my direction, said "Stanley, can't you stop her from swimming in the lake? Grandma has called her son, Jeremy, 'Stanley', ever since Stanley, my grandpa, and her husband of more than fifty years, had died not so long ago. We've all got used to the shift in names. I wandered down the drawing room, waiting for Grandma to focus on something else, and as though it were planned, I spotted a small blue book on the table in the dining room. It was called "Swimming" *by* Jabez Wolffe. Inside, it reads 'Diana Danby. Swimming Book' written in blue ink. Then there's a big scrawl in red crayon and the title printed again. "Swimming."

The next page reads as follows:

SWIMMING

Short And Long Distance

And Training

By

Jabez Wolffe

Hero Of Twenty-One Cross Channel Swims And Holder
Of Ten Long Distance Sea Records

With A Foreword By

Charles Platt

Illustrated

Revised Edition

London

W.Foulsham & Co. Ltd.

Even the size of the book is officially recorded in its pages: 5 3/4 x 3 3/4 inches. Grandma Diana said I was welcome to the book, characteristically commenting she hadn't even remembered she had it. Though I didn't study the whole thing, I did take note of an early part of the introduction which advised parents when teaching children to swim, "...place at the shallow end of the swimming bath a half-crown, and offer it to them, if they can get it up from the bottom of the bath. This they will find impossible, but at the same time it will illustrate how difficult it is to sink. Once this fact is realised, it gives them a wonderful amount of confidence." Isn't that a clever trick?! I think it is.

The swimming book, by the way, is one of a series of pocketbooks. These books were popular in their day. At the back of the "Swimming" book, there was a list of all the other books in the series. There was a sports library which included Lawn Tennis, The Game of Cricket, Golf Really Explained, How To Play Bowls Scientifically and a few more gems. Beyond the sports collection were titles including, How To Talk Correctly, 100 Varieties of Sandwiches, Constructive Thinking and How To Drive A Car Efficiently. There's no date in the book but, there is a stamp at the front that says Book Production War Economy Standard. A wonderful collection. The "Swimming" book has some basic illustrations which show, from two angles, the side view and the view from above, the form the body should take in each stroke. Though wholly charming, I still referred to the swimming content on Instagram and TikTok regularly, despite their comparatively prosaic approach.

Back at the swimming pool for a session with Jacqui, I dragged my costume on again and noticed that my legs needed waxing. It seems absurd to me now when I think back, but it was around this time that I stopped worrying about what I looked like. I'm not sure I've said that properly. I mean, I stopped thinking that I don't look 'right'. I never looked like everyone else, and all my life I'd had a subconscious thought that I should change how I looked or that somehow having pale skin and wild red hair was incorrect. Then, stripping off day after day and wearing swimsuit after swimsuit, not having time to iron my hair flat and all the tinting products failing to work when you're constantly in and out of a pool, must have subliminally forced me to embrace my natural appearance. I think I must have been in denial until then, but something just clicked. There's no such thing as an incorrect way to look. I kicked myself for not understanding this sooner. And yet I was relieved to have finally learned now instead of later... or worst of all, never!

So, back to the swimming – which I'm sure was already better as a result of my new enlightenment – I was coping sufficiently to introduce some new drills. I have to stress here, that the idea of being a proficient swimmer was still a dream. In the practical sense, that meant I had got used to the feeling of intermittently inhaling water and now felt confident that it was just unpleasant, rather than a precursor to death. Still determined to find ways to improve, it became clear that extensive drills were the natural next step.

Have you done swimming drills? If you have, you'll know there is no end to them. On this particular day, we used kick floats and tow floats. You hold the tow float between your legs when you want to concentrate on your arm technique, and you hold the kick float out in front of you when you want to concentrate on kicking. Who knows why, but I turned out to be brilliant with the kick float! It was unbelievable how fast I could go when my only task was to kick. Jacqui couldn't keep up with me as I powered up and down. It was thrilling to have identified an isolated fragment of skill. Of course, the flip side was realising how weak the rest of my swimming technique must be because I definitely couldn't zoom anywhere when my arms were involved. And sure enough, with the tow float between my legs, I wobbled along hopelessly, like a badly balanced children's bath toy. I cursed the drills for having highlighted my weaknesses so definitely.

Accepting their verdict, I turned to Instagram for more tips from the pros and buried myself in the minutiae. @swimdotcom had some good arm technique drills and I struggled not to sink the first time I tried them. I had to hold a kick float out in front with one arm and, while turned onto the side holding the float, with my other arm I had to touch the water in front, as though about to put my hand in to pull but instead of doing that, I had to lift my arm and touch the water behind me, and then to the front again. Back and forth, twice, three times was the upper limit before I lost all momentum. Then the other side. One side was worse than the other, but both were so bad it wasn't worth comparing. I concentrated furiously and hoped upon hope that the great effort would pay off.

HARRIET GOULD

Chapter 6
The Queen and Lessons

On Thursday 8th September 2022, in the afternoon, the news that had been hanging invisibly but no less certainly around us finally broke. Queen Elizabeth II had died.

I didn't know Her Majesty, but like many of us, I always felt a great closeness to her. Naturally, we have a moment of reflection at times like these. In my reflective moment, I wondered if having a Queen as the Head of State all my life is what makes me unconcerned about being a woman. It might have been the triptych of the Queen, Queen Mother and the then Prime Minister, but it has always seemed to me that women and men are equally equipped to lead. I wondered what it must be like to be born in a family that's virtually bred in captivity. How must it feel to not have a choice about the life one leads? Luckily for Queen Elizabeth II, she wasn't in line to be the monarch until events changed her destiny at the age of ten. I doubt she'd have been able to do half the things she did if she had been born next in line to the throne. I looked around the house, desperate to find something other than the copy of Sue Townsend's' "*The Queen and I*" to 'prove' I was connected to Her late Majesty. All I found was a jar of "Ma'amite."

The next morning, I went to Buckingham Palace. It was early and quite quiet. There seemed to be a lost feeling amongst those who were there. People placed their flowers along the railings, stopping briefly to think, pray, and reflect. Some flowers were wedged between the railings. The Union flag was at half-mast, barely moving in the stillness of the morning. Eventually, I turned to walk back up the path in Green Park, towards my office on Piccadilly.

Later on that same day, I went back to the Palace. It was about 5 pm and London was awake and reeling. I walked down St James Street and cut through to the path down the side of Green Park via the embassies. Walking from the Queen's Walk onto The Mall was like the difference between night and day that afternoon. The heat hit me along with the muted hum of hundreds and hundreds of people. It was reassuring in a way. I caught sight of a message on my smart watch; "Charles III address... To my darling mama, thank you for your love and devotion..." I'm not sure the late Queen could have imagined news bulletins flashing up on watch faces when she ascended the throne. I took a picture of it.

It was Sunday, 11 September, and it was time for another lesson in the lake with Val. These lakes in Little Paxton – by the way – used to be gravel pits and are now a site of national importance, so we're quite lucky to be allowed to swim there at all. This lesson was about distance...and about Val trying to convince me to swivel my head less when taking a breath. I plodded around for what felt like an eternity without the ends of the pool and the drills to break it up. That afternoon I swam 2,163 metres which seemed sufficient until I checked the conversion. It was 1.3 miles. Help! If I didn't drown on the day, maybe I'd die of boredom. Why was I doing this again? Oh yes... the medal. Why did I want that medal though? It didn't matter. I just had to swim the distance at whatever painfully slow speed I had in me. Then the blasted bike ride, but that's for another day.

I had a third and final lesson with Val the following Wednesday, September 14th, in the outdoor pool in Cambridge; yet another completely different swimming experience. Jesus Green Lido opened in August 1923 and is nearly 100 metres long. The reason it was designed to be so long, was so that swimmers could mimic swimming in the river Cam which runs alongside it. Incidentally, lidos are so-called only when they are alongside a natural body of water; otherwise, they're simply called outdoor pools. Unlike the other pools I'd been in, this one got deep in the mid-section. Deep enough for diving. Originally, the pool was fed with river water directly from the river Cam, using gravity and a weir. Thankfully, in 1956, this was converted to a closed-pump system fed with mains water because, according to Chesterton Rowing Club, "...sewage does get into the river Cam from both the outfalls of two sewage treatment plants, and from boats fitted with sea toilets...". Quick divergence onto the matter of sea "toilets" – it seems that vessels with fewer than fifteen passengers can empty their effluents at sea without breaking a single rule. Anyway, Jesus Green Lido is now as clean as it's possible to be and the only heat it draws is from the sun and the bodies swimming in it. In other words, it's cold. Not a problem in the summer, but I wore the wetsuit anyway because it seemed like another good opportunity to get used to wearing it.

In this lesson, I had to concentrate on keeping my body straight and on the length of my stroke – i.e., how efficient each stroke was. To measure the latter, Val told me to swim ten strokes, and she placed a rubber duck on the side where I had ended up. At the end of the lesson, I was to swim ten strokes again to see if I went further than where the duck was sitting. I can't tell you how lost on me all this was at the time. After two strokes, I lost count and I had no concept of distance while in the pool. Despite this, I think it was a good lesson. The photos showed me having good form, "as straight as a pencil", Val had declared, to my relief.

Two days to go. I felt a great resolution. Determined to get the job done. One good thing about having some form of competition in your past is that you retain the wherewithal to zone out of everything else, so you're not disturbed from concentrating on the task. I was in that do not disturb zone, when I saw an email saying the swim was cancelled out of respect for the late Queen. I did a double take and wondered how not getting on with anything showed any respect for the late Queen. I tried hard not to feel deflated by focusing my frustration on writing an indignant blog:

With respect

Her Majesty was stoic. She reliably got on with the job. Such was her consistency, any characterisation of her never strays from that image. It's a quality intrinsic to the British character and it is why so many Brits related to and adored her.

In the true spirit of Britishness - and as protocol and tradition dictate – we had a new monarch immediately. We are, I'm sure, grateful for the continuity, but we are still in mourning. God knows how the new monarch, King Charles III, must feel. We are reflecting on all Her Majesty represented the example she set, and the resolve she demonstrated, even in the most testing circumstances. Meanwhile, alongside the grief, His Majesty is fulfilling the duties of the monarch. We have it slightly easier. We carry on with life and fit in the occasional sombre walk to the gates of Buckingham Palace.

Life goes on. Everyone goes to work, school, on holiday. Everyone eats. We keep calm and carry on. The new monarch sees the nation calmly pulling together and feels a surge of pride and maybe even gratitude. Or so I'd imagine.

The last 24 hours suggest that we're not so stoic after all. Foodbanks and football clubs have announced they're closing. Games consoles stopped gamers from playing. Email services blocked clients. Centre Parcs and Westminster School have closed, too! "Swim Serpentine" is cancelled, although they call it 'postponed' in their email... postponed until September 2023. I'm not sure which part of Her Majesty's funeral will take place in the lake. Worst of all, medical appointments and funerals are being cancelled.

Cancelling and closing everything is the opposite of stoicism. It is the opposite of reliably getting on with the job. It is thoroughly un-British. The country is juddering to a halt. We have ceased to keep calm and nothing is carrying on. All 'out of respect' to the most reliable, unfussy, dutiful and committed Queen.

As a person has to be in their grave before they can turn in it, I feel we, the United Kingdom, have a window of opportunity to redeem ourselves and allow our beloved

Queen to rest in peace by resolving as a nation to Keep Calm and Carry On.

At the time, this felt like my only outlet and the least inappropriate way to vent. And I partly hoped that somehow someone with any say over anything might see it and change what was happening – or not happening. Sadly, no one did see it. On reflection, I realise it was arguably reasonable to cancel the swim, given the huge numbers of people involved in both activities. It would have been a bit too cluttered to have both. So I found myself in a pressure-off situation with the dreaded task still hanging over me. Instead of swimming two miles on 17 September 2022, I stood and shuffled for twelve hours in "The Queue" to pay my respects to the late Queen. It was an endurance event of sorts and wholly worth it.

Chapter 7
Treading Water

There's a Stud Farm up the road in Waresley. It used to be owned by Eddie Stibbe, the Dutch-born Olympic three-day eventer – in fact, he still claims ownership on his LinkedIn profile. A little while ago, the farm changed hands and the new owners, an enterprising pair, who weren't as horse-oriented as Eddie, decided they wanted to make different use of the 120-acre estate. One particular part includes a lake that was built – are lakes built or dug? – in the 1700s, designed along with the rest of the estate by Humphrey Repton, the landscaper known as the last great landscaper of the English landscape garden phase. The lake itself is naturally spring fed from the hills and is surrounded by ash, hazel and elegantly weeping willows. The new owners' idea was to open the lake to people who wanted to try the phenomenon of our age, 'wild swimming', a name tag that puts plenty of people on edge. I'm not sure it counts as swimming in the wild when you have to sign a disclaimer, but let's not split hairs. Before that could happen, there had to be a testing day, mainly for the promo photos I think.

Tom Ferret is the illustrious groundsman whom I met on a nighttime police stakeout when I was more directly involved in politics. Tom is impossible to turn down, and he summoned me to be part of the team of guinea pigs. Feeling bold and brave, I showed up at 7 am on Remembrance Day. The mist was still low over every part of the farm. We trucked down to the lake on Gators, through the mist and across the tracks and fields. I was driving our Gator so when we stopped, my hands were frozen to the steering wheel and I felt I'd had enough cold exposure for the day without setting foot in the lake. The side of the lake where swimmers would get in had been designed to look like a sandy beach which presented a nice juxtaposition with the mist, the sight of my breath and the marvellous iron fire pit with huge logs. Bright flames and smoke mingled with the mist. Another BBQ-style fire pit off to the side was set up for breakfast for when we'd finished, and I'm afraid the lake looked dark and ominous and menacing. Wholly uninviting.

The other guinea pigs and I stripped down to our costumes. Some sensible people had worn woolly hats and wetsuits, but I was not among them. Approaching the water's edge, my instinct was to inch my way in slowly, with Val's words in my head "Touch the water, smell the water." Then a fellow guinea pig wearing just a swimming costume casually marched forth, and I felt the pressure to keep up to save face, so I was in the lake before there was any time to touch or smell the water. Sorry, Val. The water was about ten degrees, which I'm sure was the coldest I'd experienced. According to Val, aka the lake swimming oracle, it takes the human brain 90 seconds to adjust to the conditions, so it's best to breathe normally and stay relaxed to help the brain realise there's not much to worry about. When most of us were in, we had to follow a photographer, who was in a small rowing boat, to different parts of the lake and pose. The rule of thumb is not to stay in the water for any more minutes than the number of degrees it is. So we got out after ten minutes. A splendid breakfast rustled up fireside, followed. I had to peel myself away far too soon to perform ceremonial duties at the War Memorial at St Andrew's Church in Girton, Cambridge.

I put swimming and the swim out of my mind for a few days over Christmas. Soon after Christmas, by which I mean the day after Boxing Day, I started to think about how to manage the next few months. I needed to keep ticking over in the pool but did not want to peak too soon. This way of thinking was more of a hangover from my former competitive life than a reflection of my current swimming abilities. I'm not sure what I thought 'peaking' would look like, but I am sure I needn't have worried about it. The new date for the swim had been announced as 16 September 2023. I decided I would do 'casual' swims for the time being. I didn't know exactly what I meant by that, but whatever it meant, I thought it'd give me a chance to catch up with myself and maybe deal with the niggling thought that I had been struggling to silence. The thought was that when I had had hardly any time to prepare, I could have blamed a potential poor performance on that fact. Now, with all the time in the world, I had no excuse not to produce a magnificent performance. With that in mind, I thought I'd focus a little bit more on technique and general fitness. Maybe I'd swim more often in the baby pool; the perfect place for practising new drills.

On 1 January 2023, Vicky – who I will introduce properly later – announced her intention to do a six-mile run every month for a year. I don't enjoy running nowadays, but thought it might be a good idea to join in. We were on course until a common cold struck us down in April. I hadn't thought of it before, but looking back, the six miles we ran in March was in freezing rain. Maybe something to remember. I don't mind running in the rain generally; it distracts me from the act of running. Just make sure that when you do the same, that you avoid using any products from your eyelashes upwards. Moisturiser, hair product etc., because it'll run down your face with the rain water and set fire to your eyes. I longed to refocus on swimming but stood fast with my all-around fitness plan.

As if reading my mind from across the country, an old friend from my Dorset days, Julian, rang to demand that we meet soon. I first met Julian Pritchard at a dinner party in Milton on Stour, one of those minuscule West Country villages where all the roads seem to be made of gravel and lead from one house to another. He had arrived late with two shotguns over his shoulder. We were eating pea soup. Julian is constantly under specialist physio supervision and instruction thanks to an accident he had while free running. He's lucky to be alive really. Not many people survive crashing off a building into a heap on the floor and then walking away from it. "When can we have supper?" he asked down the phone. "I'm more interested in swimming than eating", I told him. "Oh, how exciting! We can go for a swim then!" The extraordinary thing about learning to swim is finding out how many other people already swim and do it regularly in our midst. It's like joining a club that I didn't know existed. A Secret Swimmers Club. I met Julian after work, and from his flat in Earls Court we bundled into his tatty old Golf GTI to make our way to his club.

Another 'best' thing about swimming is how little room it takes up. I mean, if I were to go for a run, I would have to lug trainers along, as well as all the clothes. With swimming, the items are tiny and practically fit in your pocket, so you can be ready to swim all the time! I sometimes found myself daydreaming about how good swimming is – somewhat of a departure from where I began. The speed bumps snapped me out of that train of thought and I focused on what I could see out of the window: Earls Court has always felt like home to me. Apart from being born up the road, at Queen Charlotte's Hospital, which I don't remember, I worked at the glorious Exhibition Centre in my earliest twenties. It wasn't an especially brilliant job, but the offices were arranged on the upper floors around the central stadium area... a bit like hospitality boxes, only without the view. This arrangement came into its own when people were rehearsing for their concerts. Some artists were very good sports and didn't mind us sneaking in for a private viewing. I was told that Madonna hadn't been so keen on that. I'm sorry to say I wouldn't know because I wasn't there when she'd been in the house. Earl's Court Exhibition Centre was built in 1935 and had an 'internal' swimming pool to "rival any other in the world". The pool, or "basin" as it was known, was 60 metres long and 30 metres wide and took 2.25 million gallons of water and four days to fill it. Emptying it took the same amount of time. It was filled every year for the London Boat Show so that the Sunseekers, Oceancos and Princess Yachts could be shown off in their natural environment. Unfortunately for me, the London Boat Show had moved to The Excel Centre by the time I had anything to do with it. When the pool wasn't in use, a retractable floor that weighed 750 tonnes covered it to form the show floor for year-round concerts and exhibitions.

Before the exhibition centre was built, the land was marked out by the ever-expanding railway network and before that, Earl's Court was farmland attached to Earl's Court Manor. The new owners of this isolated plot commissioned C. Howard Crane, the American theatre architect to design the imposing new building. Earl's Court Exhibition Centre opened on 1 September 1937 and the first exhibition was the Chocolate and Confectionary Show.

Earl's Court Exhibition Centre was a mere seventy-four years old – arguably in her prime – when she was razed to the ground in 2014. The destruction had been signed off by the then Mayor of London, Boris Johnson. I try and eliminate knowledge of the demolition from my consciousness. Thanks to various relationship ructions between developers and councils – or those who control the councils – ground is yet to be broken on the site and the hoarding is still up.

The other reason that Earls Court feels like home is because Great Auntie Fay and Great Uncle John lived there. One day, sitting at the table in their kitchen – which was ochre – it occurred to me that I didn't know where they would park if they had a car; theirs was a mansion flat on Trebovir Road and parking was scarce. "Do you drive?" I asked Auntie Fay. "No! Darling!" She gasped, "I drink!". It didn't stop her from doing anything else, so I'm surprised it stopped her from driving. To call her adventurous doesn't go far enough. She learned to belly dance in her forties and demonstrated this once on a table in a restaurant. She wore stilettos in the snow and would go on jaunts with her neighbours to Russia, China and anywhere else she found interesting – and she'd learn the language. Great Uncle John would go, too, when he had time off. John was a Doctor. A General

Practitioner and one of the first NHS Doctors ever, which in those days equated to being a local celebrity. John died at age 94 in 2015 and Fay died at age 94, two years after that. At their house-leaving party, held in their honour with family, neighbours and friends present, I delivered the reading as Fay had performed it at John's funeral. If I had just read it out, it would have been meaningless. I had to set the scene and I will do the same now. The funeral was held in a Synagogue in North London. It was freezing and so dark inside. Fay, then 92, petite and wrapped up in fur pelts, made her way slowly in a low heel across the stone floor and up to the pulpit. Her voice was pure light. By which I don't mean soft, I mean with her voice she lit the place up with vibrancy and force. I imitated her in the room of people. This is what she said:

So, I was left alone all night

     with my dead lover.

No, never dead, forever living.

70 years of loving and belonging.

That will never leave me.

Memories sustaineth,

Comfort evermore,

That will never leave me,

That I know for sure.

We arrived at the club at dusk. It felt as though we were at the grand gates of a Stepford-esque promised land. We drove along the driveway, tennis courts on the left and trees and I think a lake on the right. Julian parks with a running commentary that includes reference to every single animate and inanimate object within a ten-metre radius of his chosen space. When I park, I just sling the car wherever it fits. Inside, the pool seemed wide compared to its length. It was divided in two for no reason that I could make out. The water was perfectly comfortable but too warm for an energetic swim. The whole pool was quite shallow, which made it seem as if I was going faster than I was. I can't work out if that happens or if it's an illusion. I still braced myself for seeing the sight of the bottom of the pool, but miraculously no longer felt scared. I enjoyed inspecting what was down there. The tiles were quite dark blue and small and seemed to sparkle a little. We split the time between swimming, steaming and sauna-ing. The chat in the sauna was mainly hostile and aimed at either the Mayoral Office, the Royal Borough of Kensington and Chelsea Council the Borough of Hammersmith and Fulham Council, or all three, for tampering with the local speed limits. I lay back and inhaled deeply through my nose. Afterwards, we chucked our things in the car and went back inside for supper. This is surely the best thing about swimming here – the chance to eat in a real restaurant immediately after swimming without having to go anywhere else. And now I know what 'casual' swimming means. Thumbs up for the Hurlingham Club.

Over Christmas 2022, a good friend's girlfriend died, suddenly and unexpectedly. It was awful and he was devastated. His brother, Luke, desperate to give him a reason to get out of bed, suggested a few of us should aim to swim one mile in the Jesus Green Lido, a thing I wouldn't have ordinarily been able to do, having not been able to swim. So you can imagine the bittersweet pleasure of being able to take part. We were eight altogether and via the "April Showers 1 Mile Swim" WhatsApp group we agreed a date – 22 April – and updated each other with our training and progress reports.

It was quite cold when the date rolled around. The water was 12 degrees centigrade. Trying not to think too much about it, I grabbed my wetsuit and made my way to the pool. I was a bit late. Naomi had waited for me. Naomi Bateman is one of the super swimmers and one of my closest and oldest friends. She used to compete in and win swimming galas. We spent our primary school years being sent to the 'red mat' together. The red mat was a reddish carpet tile on the floor in the corridor outside the staff room. It was the naughty step of the day before the advent of Super Nanny. I can't remember a single reason for being sent to the red mat, but I can remember how much we enjoyed discussing important matters while we were on it, as well as getting glimpses of the inside of the staff room to see who was smoking.

Primary school days behind us, we got into the pool, (Naomi with her usual sound effects). Off we went. It was too cold initially to think about much, so I just made sure I concentrated on keeping count of the lengths. Remember, this pool is nearly 100 meters long, so it'd be especially easy to lose count along the way. After a while, I warmed up nicely and the freshness of the water was a joy. It's like pressing a master reset button when you're pushing your face along through the cold water, plus it keeps you at a reasonable temperature, countering the heat generated by the effort of swimming. It wasn't until the very last length that the balance tipped and the cold started to have an effect. And the last half of the last length was really hard; my hands had started to cramp into a kind of claw shape. Fortunately, there's a – quite small – sauna which we all squashed into in a rowdy heap to warm up. We were the only ones there. Can't imagine why.

That evening, I drove to Barnet to stay the night with Grandma Greta. I was taking her to Bexhill On Sea the following day. Her friends, David and Stephen live there and they hadn't seen each other since the pandemic stopped their regular meetings at the National Theatre. More recently, Stephen had become ill, and they all worried they wouldn't be together again. When Grandma mentioned this, it seemed obvious that I could just give her a lift to see them. It was 98 miles from Barnet to Bexhill and 98 miles back. Grandma pointed out on the way there that even our drive wasn't as far as the bike ride I still hadn't started preparing for!

Chapter 8
On Two Wheels

Just like starting to swim, I'm embarrassed to say what I'm sure you already know by now. Yes - I had been putting it off. I had even put off getting a bike until the eleventh hour, too. My first defence is that I felt over-confident – possibly because I could already ride a bike and, having learned to swim, I felt as though anything, even a 100-mile bike ride was simple. My second defence is that choosing a bike is worse than riding a million miles. The choice is huge, and the bike is just the obvious bit you need.

When you start with nothing, there seems to be an endlessness to the number of items you need for a bike ride. After much (too much?) research, I settled for a TREK AL2. In blue. It was in a sale and still cost more than I would have ever dreamed of spending on a bike. And then the rest of the kit. I followed the advice on everything. The advice came mainly from Gareth. Gareth Crapper used to run the labs at Akzo Nobel and has since transformed himself into a cycle tour guide in the Peak District, so at least he knows what's what. Gareth told me all about padded 'bib' shorts, shoes, socks, vests, and jerseys. I've put a short kit list at the end of this book for reference.

My entire prep for this bike ride was possibly the opposite of the great effort I made – or had to make – for swimming. I did five training rides altogether. Ride one, on 8 May, was in a thunderstorm, and I was soaked through after two minutes. I did 20 miles. The next ride was in town with my friend, Harry. We cycled about 20 miles then as well. I wore normal clothes and so did he. Harry Mount is a journalist. We met at the bonfire party of a particularly generous friend whose plan to set us up, I'm afraid, didn't work. Harry and I cycled a route around the Wren Churches, a route that he'd wanted to check in preparation for a tour he was giving to readers of "The Oldie." Harry is the editor of this magazine, so it was especially important he gets the route right. The wonderful thing about cycling with Harry is that he pays no attention to anything other than where he wants to go. There may as well not be any lanes, lines or lights at all. What's more, it turns out Harry had himself done this beastly bike ride. "What did you wear?!" I asked him, not being able to imagine him in anything resembling a cycling get-up. "This" he replied, looking confused and gesturing down at his chino, shirt, and jacket uniform.

After that, PTJoolz got involved with her husband, also called Jules, who takes cycling a little bit seriously. Jules taught me how to use the gears properly. After our last ride together, he issued tactics; "aim to stick at 14 mph" he said and lent me a speedometer to have on my bike, so I would have half a chance of sticking to his instruction.

I had booked two nights at the Farmers Club on Whitehall Court, thinking I might appreciate a local bed after the ride as well as before. And, as it turned out, the front door was two hundred yards from the start line.

When I arrived to check in, the man at the desk noticed I had a bike at the heel and invited me to park it in the basement. I thanked him but instead took it down to my room, thinking ahead to getting ready in the morning. The downside of this club is that you can't get fed at the weekend. It turned out to be an upside though, thanks to Deliveroo! I ordered a delicious pasta something or other, from a wonderful restaurant in Waterloo called Al Dente. The bedroom had a single bed. I couldn't remember what single beds had looked like all my life, but this one looked so narrow that you'd need great skill to balance on it all night. First, I laid out the million items of clothing and kit in the order I'd need them. Then, preferring a flat surface, I pushed the pillows onto the floor, lay back on the balance beam of a bed and went to sleep.

28 May 2023, I woke up at 6 am and was ready to go soon afterwards. I'd forgotten about organising breakfast, but luckily there was a packet of two biscuits in the room. I shoved them in my jersey pocket and left. Masses of people – hundreds – were queuing across the end of Whitehall Court, astride their bikes in various ways and wearing every colour and cycling fashion known to man. I tottered along to join them. Tottering because of the 'cleats' on my cycling shoes. Cleats, by the way, must be bought separately from the shoes themselves... and from the pedals. But it's a good idea to buy pedals, shoes and cleats at the same time, so you can make sure they all fit one another. I've no idea if I was in the correct "start wave" but it didn't seem to matter. After a little while, there was an elongated clicking sound caused by the hundreds of people clipping their cleated shoes onto their pedals, and then the herd moved. We crossed the start line and I remembered to start my watch, hoping the battery would last out.

Off we rode, along Embankment in stunningly fresh and bright morning sun. I made a point of enjoying the view while I could. The river was glinting in the sun and soon enough Canary Wharf gleamed ahead. In a blink, we turned sharply to the left, aiming north toward Stratford, then back down to Bow, then up and around Hackney. At some point, there was a crash, slightly ahead of where I was. The herd stopped, and I ate one of my biscuits. We set off after a few minutes and were onto Epping New Road for a long straight run uphill.

The first stop was at the 25-mile point, Epping. It looked chaotic and I didn't stop because I couldn't think of a reason to. By 50 the mile point, at Great Dunmow, I was ready to refill my water bottles and go to the loo. There were bike racks to park at. Having tied my treasured steed up with Grandma Diana's old bike lock, I traipsed in the no-longer fresh heat, across a playing field to the even hotter portaloos. It was my least favourite loo stop of all time. The safety pins holding the 'race' number on went through too many layers of garments, and over-the-shoulder bib shorts were involved, so working out what was moveable took an age. The water station straight ahead of the loos on the other side of the playing field was diagonally opposite the only place that had food. The food on offer was crates and crates of bananas, all cut in half. I got two halves and ate them on the way to the water station. Back at the bike, I added electrolytes to the water and got back on my way. There was a little queue to get out, so I ate my other biscuit.

Not long afterwards, there was another crash. By now it was searingly hot, and I hadn't thought to take sunblock, so I asked the people around me if they had any.

Fortunately, someone had. I squirted it all over and thanked him profusely from the safety of a single patch of shade cast by a convenient oak tree on the verge. Then the herd were off again.

At mile 75, I stopped at a garage for more water. I also got an ice cream and a packet of crisps – which I ate immediately – and a Star Bar which I stowed in the little pocket at the back of my seat for when I'd finished.

The last time the herd stopped before the finish was at a junction. I could see all the stopping up ahead and unclipped my right foot in preparation. As the bike slowed to a stop, it started to fall to the left, towards my unclipped foot. Thankfully, I didn't miss a beat, unclipping and planting my left foot down in what can only have been a nanosecond, catching the bike at just over the 45-degree point. It must have looked good from behind.

In the last 20 miles or so, there were the best downhill runs – top speed 39mph – and some tiresome climbs. At the 97-mile sign, the balls of my feet began to burn.

Finally, I was across Tower Bridge and over the finish line. My friend, Penny, and various members of the Brown family were there that day. Penny and her son Simon were at the finish line having cheered Penny's other son, William, a personal trainer, home earlier and were waiting for Penny's husband, Andrew, to finish after me, so I got all their attention in the meantime.

As soon as I was over the line and around the corner, I got off the bike and took my shoes off. Penny and Simon were right there on the other side of the railings, so I gave the shoes to Penny and lifted my bike over the barrier to Simon. I plodded off with my Star Bar to get my medal.

A medal is an odd thing in this context because they are basically souvenirs, acknowledging your entry in and completion of the event. Given that, it's nice when the organisers or sponsors indulge the entrants by providing splendid medals. The 2021 Virgin Money London Marathon medal was super. It had good substance, was round, a decent size and the ribbon was well-designed, so it sat well when being worn. This medal was only one of those things: round. It was made of very light wood, so it didn't feel at all satisfying to hold and didn't hang well. At least I stuck to the plan of keeping at 14mph, and I only had one part of the London Classics challenge to go.

The morning after, I'd never been so hungry. There aren't many places to get food nearby on what was a Bank Holiday Monday. I settled for Starbucks. After refuelling, I packed up and started to make my way home. I'd read something about a 'recovery ride' being a good idea, so I hopped on the bike, crossed Whitehall, crunched over the gravel in Horse Guards Parade, then rolled down The Mall and up to Green Park tube. They wouldn't let me take my bike through the turnstiles – bikes weren't allowed. I'm glad my journey into town wasn't disrupted by this rule. Anyway, the woman guarding the station told me I'd have to go back to Victoria because it was a hybrid station. I backed away and, in a silent act of rebellion to her instruction, cycled to Finsbury Park instead. It only took about 30 minutes, but it was more cycling than I'd hoped to ever have to do again.

I was hungry for about two weeks after the bike ride and my neck hurt so much that even swimming didn't help, so

I sought intervention from Lucy, the most excellent physio who happens to live moments away from me. Lucy Haith was formerly responsible for keeping the prima ballerinas at the Royal Ballet up and running. When I arrived, Lucy poked at the muscles around my shoulders. "Phwoar! Has Joolz been making you throw weights around again?" She hadn't, as it happened. I wondered what to say to explain myself for a moment before remembering, "Oh! It's probably the swimming! I had to learn to swim!"

HARRIET GOULD

Chapter 9
Maintenance, Moles and Momentum

By mid-June, I had finally recovered from the bike ride and the country was turning into an oven. Over Christmas 2022, PTJoolz told me that she'd ordered a LUMI plunge pod. You probably know that these are little ice baths that you can set up in your garden. You fill them with cold water and add ice if you want to. The idea is you sit in it every morning and stay there for a few minutes. When I found out that she was getting one, I felt left out and ordered one immediately. It stayed in its box by the back door for two weeks before I put it in the garage.

My plan to use the plunge pod that winter was stalled by little things, mainly the low, low temperature. But then, as spring broke, I realised I didn't have a hosepipe. I know it's easy enough to go and buy one (as almost everyone told me) but I had a vivid vision of disused hosepipes piling up across the nation, hundreds of them. Down alleys, in sheds and garages and neglected in corners of gardens. What's more, I felt sure I could restore a dormant pipe to life. So when my friend, Vicky, of too many years to mention, summoned me to help with a yard sale in her village, I saw my opportunity.

Vicky Parsons is an outlier among the close friends because she does not swim. She, too, had suffered from ineffective lessons at school. Nevertheless, I consider Vicky very much part of the learn-to-swim team because of her constant encouragement and endless bolstering.

At the village sale, in one person's yard, all kinds of plants and associated gardening paraphernalia were for sale. I asked if they had a hosepipe and the woman swore about having three and forgetting to bring a single one of them. Luckily, she lived nearby, so I arranged to go and collect one of them and felt extremely satisfied.

It was so hot by now that I was bursting to try my new plunge pod. With my adopted hosepipe installed, I set up the pod, perching it on top of a wooden pallet and using old election boards as padding. So the next day, I braved the chill and got into the pod. It felt wonderful. The only problem was how much I wanted to lie in the garden all day after using it. I fell into a terrific morning routine of going out for a walk, then straight into the plunge pod. Every day, the water felt freezing, and it seemed impossible; yet every day I did it and ended up enjoying it. Something about the stillness of the water and the reflection of the clouds and disorderly wisteria branches was hypnotic. Looking down and up at the same time gave me a great sense of gratitude for my surroundings. The feeling was so good that I suddenly realised that happiness transcends events. And it still seems impossible to me, that before I learned to swim, I found entering even slightly cooler water practically out of the question and now look! I was voluntarily getting into ice-cold water and, what's more, enjoying it!

Then it was July, and the sun blazed down like it used to when I was small. I felt fresh from the cold plunging and from wearing next to nothing all day with a fan on. All was well. One afternoon, I noticed a mole on my left arm, and I couldn't be sure whether I had seen it before. In an instant, I was making calculations to see if I'd still have enough time to train and swim if I had the mole removed. It did cross my mind to ignore it until after the swim, but I concluded that there were probably some very good waterproof plasters around these days. I know that this may seem like an overreaction – and I have been known to overreact – but in the case of cancerous moles, I have form.

In 2017, my doctor sent me to the skin specialist at Addenbrooke's Hospital to have a mole on my arm removed and tested.

Cancerous moles are sometimes called melanoma and sometimes not because a malignancy can occur where there is no mole. The severity of a melanoma is measured by depth or thickness.

Melanomas grow downwards, into the arm or other parts of the body. You can spot them because they look irregular in shape, colour and undulation. Not all moles with irregular characteristics are cancerous, however.

This test revealed that the mole in question was the thinnest version of melanoma – 0.05mm thin. Despite this, it was necessary to excavate the area around the site of where the mole had been, in order to search for stray cells. Luckily for me, the cells had conformed to the vertical trend, so all of them had been removed in the first dig.

It was quite a big excavation area, which took weeks to heal and years to stop hurting.

Given the sunny prognosis, this may not seem like a big ordeal; but it does serve to remind us of the obvious. We are vulnerable as individuals and life really might be quite short.

I suppose it's easier not to dwell on that, but I don't think there's anything wrong with considering our mortality occasionally. We're not entitled to a long, healthy life, although we might get one. So thinking about how to make the most of it probably isn't a bad thing.

If this happens to you, these are the things I think are important to remember. Having moles removed can be addictive. I had eight removed after the bad mole, and the last one put me off. It was directly where nearly every waistband sits, which made the healing process much longer.

The next thing to remember is that scarred skin is less good at being skin than non-scarred skin, so the less scarred skin you have, the better.

Finally, you have to go back for "mole mapping." This means having your moles photographed once a year for three years. Some moles are measured and monitored for changes. After the third mole mapping, if there are no changes, you'll likely have reached the end of what's known as the cancer pathway.

I hope you can forgive my overreaction now that you know the context. As it turned out, the newly detected mole wasn't anything sinister, so I could carry on with the business of swimming without another thought.

The business of swimming continued in Cambridge when Naomi suggested we train together one day. Other than the April Showers swim in the Jesus Green Lido, and splashing around on holidays and at school, this was the first time Naomi and I had swum properly together.

The Cambridge Nuffield pool is much smarter than the St Albans equivalent, but the pool is warmer and only has three lanes. I walked Naomi through the pre-swim routine that Jacqui had taught me. The main feature was to wet the hair in the shower before the chlorine touched it. Wetting the hair seals the shaft, which in turn protects it from the pool water. I was desperate to see if I could keep up with Naomi in an indoor pool. I felt so sure I would be able to, despite never being able to keep up with Jacqui, and Naomi was a competitive swimmer. So it's likely that you guessed before I told you that I certainly couldn't keep up with her. When we did leg drills, she left me for dust. You've never seen anything so magnificently powerful in a casual swim setting.

July being nearly over was one thing. August being about to start was another matter and focused my mind again. On 28 July I happened to be in town for one thing and another. One thing was one side of Hyde Park and the other thing was the other side of Hyde Park, so I decided I would walk through the park and test the water on the way. I mean this literally. You can't swim in the Serpentine any time you feel like it, but you can swim in the Serpentine Lido at almost any time and have been able to since 1930. George Lansbury was the person responsible for its development, and there's a plaque commemorating his efforts on the wall in the lido café.

It costs £5 to swim in the lido, plus £2 if you use a locker, as I did. The lockers and changing rooms are in the clubhouse across the path from the entrance to the side of the lake where the lido is situated. The Serpentine Lido isn't really a lido. It's a segment of the lake, with a string of grubby white buoys slung around its edge, to mark it out from the rest of the water. It's roughly rectangular, about 100 metres long and is very much part of the lake.

On this day, the pool was empty of people, which didn't fill me with enthusiasm. Plus, the weather was cloudy and grey and not especially warm. To reinforce the point, there was a blackboard with the water temperature chalked on it. '19C' it said.

Standing at the edge put me off. The water looked uninviting and a bit dirty. At least it wasn't ominously still like the Waresley lake. There were ripples to contend with in the Serpentine Lido. The whole land edge of the rectangle was a slope into the pool, and there were handrails at intervals along its length. At one end, there was a jetty with a smart set of silver steps. I looked around for moral support. The Head Lifeguard, Simon, came to my aid. I asked him about the water, the ground, the people who'd usually be there and why they weren't there today. He explained that the slope was slippery, the water was tested for bacteria every week and for the dreaded blue-green algae and people generally weren't as keen on swimming when the weather was grim.

Finally, Simon pointed out the shower zone. A pair of single silver pipes standing over small plug holes. He told me no soap or washing substance of any sort could be used because it would get into the lake and upset the ecology. And don't assume – as I did – that there are showers in the locker rooms because there aren't.

I went over to get changed, and in passing realised how much more adaptable I'd become. Before I started swimming, I'd always been thrown off balance by the unexpected or the new. I probably still was, but I seemed to be finding ways to function normally at the same time. Costume on, hat and goggles in hand, I walked back across the path, between the people, through the gate and to the shower for the hair-wetting process. The water from the shower was stone-cold, and, as I stood there in the freezing flow, I wondered for the millionth time, how I was doing any of this.

The sloping edge wasn't too slippery after all. I walked in confidently and got my head under the water quickly. It didn't have the same fresh, pure smell as the Little Paxton lake. It was more musty. The worst thing was how murky it was. For the first few strokes, I felt like a brand-new swimmer all over again. Not being able to see through the water is so disorientating. It was a similar feeling to trying to walk with your eyes closed. Green things that looked like filaments hung in the water. At least it was organic, whatever it was.

I kept looking up to check that I was swimming in a straight line. Looking up in swimming is called 'sighting' and is a specific technique. A technique I hadn't practised and that I would certainly need to practice!

Another thing to consider when you're sharing a lake with birds is to check for feathers when turning your head to take a breath. At last, I got into a bit of a rhythm, despite the myriad new obstacles. As though to counter the less-than-satisfactory experience, there was a glorious smell of bacon drifting across the water from the café.

I got out with bacon rolls in my sights. First I rinsed as thoroughly as I could in the cold, soapless shower. Then I zipped a fellow swimmer into their wetsuit before returning to the locker room. I had a tiny T-shirt-type towel to help squeeze my hair a bit dry.

I got dressed and trying not to salivate in anticipation, I rushed next door to the café for bacon. Unfortunately, they'd just stopped serving, so I had to make do with a massive almond croissant, which I ate on a bench beside the lido. Four or five geese joined me, pecking up all the pastry flakes that I kept dropping.

For about a month or so, at least until I tested the Serpentine water, I'd had romantic notions of living near the lake and swimming in it every day. I moved on from that whimsical idea once I'd tested the water. My new aspiration became having a nice clean pool nearby. In truth, I wished that I would never have to set foot in the Serpentine ever again. It was a similar feeling to the feeling I had when I began trying to swim in the first place. 'How am I ever going to learn to swim' had become 'How am I ever going to swim two miles in that lake'. I realised at that moment just how much clear progress I'd made. I paused and thought back to see if I could pinpoint the exact moment when I had learned to swim, and I couldn't. Instead, as with most things in life, the more you do something, the better you get at it. I continued to marvel at this concept as I returned to the flat in Málaga two days later. Swimming in the sea was no longer an ordeal but a treat, especially when the fish came to play.

Once again, it was nice to be back from the beach and into the pool, but these days, only because of the functional benefit rather than avoiding the fear factor. On this occasion, my usual pool was 'closed for maintenance', so I went to the Nuffield pool in Letchworth, which is much closer to where I live. It occurred to me that if this pool was as good as the St Albans pool, I would have no choice but to make this my go-to pool.

At first glance, the building gives out care home vibes. A relatively new red-brick building and gable windows. The sort of building across which I could imagine ivy making good progress. Inside, it felt similar to the Cambridge Nuffield gym, with a fresh feeling, like a spa.

The lockers were not straightforward. In Biggleswade, the lockers have a municipal-issue key and wrist strap. The same with the Jesus Green Lido lockers in Cambridge. The Cambridge Nuffield is a key with a safety pin. In St Albans, you have a choice of either a key with a safety pin or using your own padlock. I chose a padlock, to avoid faffing with a safety pin. The Hurlingham club lockers are operated by a code, which you choose yourself by following the simple instructions on the door, and it's the same at the Letchworth Nuffield, except the process is more complicated. It took several attempts to make it work and, according to others in the changing room, this was typical of these temperamental lockers.

Eventually, I stowed my stuff, found the showers to wet my hair and opened the door to the pool. This is the only place where I've had to open the door to get to the pool. Everywhere else had a maze of walls, and in the cases where there were doors, they were always propped open. The poolroom felt warm. I picked a workout sheet, hoping the water would contrast with the air.

Workout sheets are another feature of the Nuffield pools. They have various swimming workouts, where you can choose from 10 to about 120 lengths. Each sheet breaks down the workout into four stages: warm-up, stroke development, main set and cool down. Some of the workouts incorporate floats for stroke development, otherwise known as drills. I usually aimed to swim about a mile, which is about 60 lengths of a 25-metre pool. I took my workout sheet to the end of the pool and slid into the water. It was warm! Warmer than any other pool! Far too warm for anything energetic. Almost too warm for a casual swim! I tried my best. Luckily, there was an open shower by the pool which spurted out ice-cold water. It was so warm that I couldn't even wear my swimming hat. I used the ice shower after every few lengths to stop myself from bursting into flames in the same way you have to cool down in between sauna sessions. It was probably quite healthy in some ways but made it hard to do decent mileage there.

In August, with only four weeks to go until the event itself, I took casual swimming to a new realm. Naomi had arranged a short break at her new retreat, Fritton Lakes, which is a part of the Somerleyton Estate, on the border of Norfolk and Suffolk. We thought playing in the Fritton lake would be a good precursor to swimming in the Serpentine.

Fritton Lake was born out of a more practical need. It was dug out in medieval times, specifically to extract peat to be used as fuel. When it had flooded, it was used as a bird decoy for hunting waterfowl - a miserable practice where channels were dug and ducks encouraged to paddle along them, only to be trapped in nets at the end.

Later on, during World War II, it was used as a secret training site. The lake's origins contrast completely with the ambitious mission of its current custodians, Lord Crossley, 4th Baron Somerleyton and his Wife, Lady Crossley, to re-wild over half of the Somerleyton Estate. One half of the lake is in Norfolk and the other half is in Suffolk, not that there was any difference between the two halves.

There was a floating sauna on the lake, which felt luxurious and made the lake incredibly appealing. Having worked up a decent sweat, we jumped into the bottomless lake, which I purposely didn't think about. I hadn't taken goggles either, so looking was out of the question. We swam about a hundred yards to a duck poo-encrusted pontoon, then we swam back to the sauna and so on. After two days of swimming in and paddle-boarding on the lake and floating in the pool, I felt like I'd been away for a year.

HARRIET GOULD

Chapter 10
Countdown

With three weeks to go, I started to visualise swimming the two-mile route, with the knowledge that each lap was one mile. This meant I would have to go round twice, surrounded by hundreds of other people doing the same thing.

When I went back to the pool in St Albans to do yet more lengths, I wondered how to recreate the feeling of swimming in a crowded environment because, despite having swum in more pools than I ever imagined possible, as well as swimming in four lakes and the sea – all unquestionably valuable experience – none of it had prepared me for being crowded or swum into.

I asked Jacqui if she'd mind swimming into me in a disruptive way, but she was afraid I'd injure her, and I'm not surprised. It'd be like asking her little mermaid to swim into the path of my massive tramp steamer.

The next day in the pool, as though by divine intervention, there were two men in the lane beside me. They steamed up and down like machine-powered vessels. When they stopped, I took my chance. My new amphibious friends were called Ford and Adrian, and they both obliged and even seemed to enjoy my request. For 20 lengths or so, we recreated a range of crowded swimming scenarios. During one of these, Adrian grabbed my ankles while Ford swam at my hip, smashing his arm down by my face on every stroke. Then we'd switch and Ford would slow down dramatically in front of me while Adrian would shoot past, sending a wave over my head... and so on. It felt wholly chaotic. Satisfied that I was well-conditioned for whatever conflict I might face on the day, we went to the sauna, the two of them having firmly earned a place on my learn-to-swim team. Ford went on to warn me that I might get swum over. He said race swimmers are merciless and suggested I wear spare goggles around my neck, just in case.

On 1 September, there were sixteen days to go, and I concentrated on nourishing myself with what I believe to be the three most important aspects of any athletic endeavour: food, stretching and sleep. Last year at this stage, even though my swimming was far weaker and slower, I was regularly swimming at least 90 lengths in the 25-metre pool. This time around, I barely went over 50 lengths. Back then, I felt terrified of not being able to make it round the two-mile course. The contrast with how I felt this time was stark. This time, I felt confident and almost sorry that it might seem less of a challenge. As though somehow I'd cheated the challenge by improving so much. I felt no need to constantly prove to myself that I was capable; I knew I had nothing to worry about.

12th September, four days to go, and an email arrived from the organisers. The subject line read, "Important Update". It was a notice to warn us that the event could yet be cancelled because there'd been a "bloom" of blue-green algae. There wasn't much to do apart from kick myself for not ticking the refundable box for the room I'd just booked at the Hub by Premier Inn. The email said that we would be told if the swim would go ahead by 17.00hrs the following day.

The time came and went with no update. I tried not to think about it, but I couldn't help it! What would happen if they cancelled it again? I dreaded the idea of waiting another whole year but concluded that it didn't matter either way, because at least I would never have to learn to swim from scratch again. In a way, I had already done my challenge. Nevertheless, I assumed that whenever news came, it would be good news.

The next day, we were informed via the Facebook Group that the latest test results showed a decrease in the "levels". There was a more technical update via email, which included the number of algae cells per ml measure, along with a graph that showed low, medium and high levels, and pointed out the World Triathlon limit, which is on the line between medium and high. Finally, on 14th September, it was confirmed, that the team were satisfied that the blue-green algae bloom was under control, and it would be safe to swim.

It was all systems go. Again.

HARRIET GOULD

Chapter 11
The Swim

I checked into the tiny hotel on Dacre Street, Westminster, at about 20:00 and ordered supper. There was a choice of pizza or chicken curry. I chose the latter. It was surprisingly perfect.

On the day, I showered first thing, then wondered why. After breakfast, I got an UBER to the park and waited for James on the Serpentine Bridge.

James Poole is my cousin. We rarely see each other and apart from a longish weekend in Florence, the longest we had ever spent together was a week in Lagrasse, helping Granny Mary and Grandpa John clean up the devastation, after the river L'Orbieu, the main vein running through the Languedoc region, which ran along the edge of their land, had forked a few kilometres upstream, taking a new and destructive route through their garden. James had generously agreed to be my bag carrier for the morning. While I waited, I took a photo of the lake. The swimmers were minute against the huge buoys and the vast expanse of the lake, which had always seemed quite a reasonable sized until this morning.

James arrived with Marmite the dog in tow, and we found a shady patch between the trees to wait for my start time. It turned out my only cue to start was the time, so at 09:45 I began to get ready. I already had my costume on, so I just swapped my shorts and shirt for my wetsuit. I gave James my most important item; the wristband that I would need at the finish to collect the London Classics medal.

Conveniently, there had been a complimentary bottle of water in the hotel room, which I'd brought along and now used to drench my hair. Discussing swimming credentials, James confirmed that it did not look as if this was my first time at a swimming event. He even ventured that – thanks to the protective water – this could easily have been my seventh or eighth time.

I left James and Marmite with my bag and followed the signs to the start. There were hundreds of us. We were corralled into sections beside the lake and then filtered through smaller gateways, where we had to scan the tag that every swimmer wore, secured with Velcro around the ankle. I scanned mine and entered the final holding zone, with all the other seal-like neoprene-clad bodies.

The sun was intense, even at 10:00, so I found a spot of shade to sit in. I could hear a commentator shouting excitedly over the PA system, but I wasn't listening. Instead, I was studying the water and the route into the water. Up ahead, I could see a floating walkway to the left. People walked along it then turned left again and went down a 45-degree angled ramp that looked no more than a metre long, and they were off! There certainly wasn't space or time for touching nor for smelling the water.

The water itself looked worse than it had done when I tested it in August. Today it looked more brown than green. I vowed not to swallow a single drop. At least two people had advised me to drink a can of Coke before and after the swim to kill accidentally ingested germs. So I researched this, and it turns out that the only reason we're able to drink Coke in the first place is that stomach acid is more powerful, ie, our bodies are better at killing lake germs than anything else would be. At least that had been one fewer thing to worry about.

The ominous moment arrived. The people in front of me began to shuffle towards the raft walkway. At that moment, I felt utterly incredulous that I had diminished the vastness of this challenge. Halfway to the floating walkway, I put my special event-issued hat on and was glad I'd had the foresight to bring that bottle of water to wet my hair. As I stepped onto the walkway, I put my goggles on. My face was a bit wet from the bottle of water, but the goggles were dry. Usually, I'd put the goggles on in the water and test that I'd got them on correctly, to make sure no water would get in. But there was no time for all that, so I put them on and hoped for the best.

We were moving at more than a shuffle now, and I was at the end of the walkway. It was time to turn left and go down the ramp. I made an effort to stride forth with conviction, pretending it was the millionth time I'd done it, rather than the first. I launched myself from the end of the ramp into the lake as seamlessly as I could, pushing off the ramp as though it were the wall of a swimming pool.

The water was cold enough for me to be glad that I wore my wetsuit – unbelievably, this hadn't been a given. My mission was simple: swim up the lake, go around the buoys at the end, swim down the lake, go around the buoys at the other end, swim up the lake past the start line and repeat. Three strokes in, I realised that my first challenge was to fathom out where I was and where I needed to be. The course was easier to see from outside the water.

From the water level, it was hard to get my bearings, especially when peering through the murkiness. I don't think I could have seen my hand at the end of my outstretched arm in the water ahead of me, because it was so murky. I was trying to get into a good rhythm, so when I lifted my head in my first attempt to see where I was going, I saw immediately that I was off course, veering to the left, over to the edge of the lake. I corrected myself and carried on.

The next time I looked, I had gone too far the other way. There was no danger of accidentally swimming into the centre of the lake because people were prowling around the inside of the course in kayaks. They moved surprisingly nimbly into position, to block any poor stray swimmer in their tracks. I took a moment longer with my head up to locate the furthest point I should be aiming for and saw that the end buoys were purple and far bigger than the interim yellow buoys, so I lined myself up with a purple buoy and got going again. The good thing about the navigation turning out to be so technical was that this became my overriding focus and all other anticipated concerns evaporated.

As I got to the top of the lake for the first time, I glanced around to see if some terrifying power pack of a swimmer was about to swim over me. There was no one there, so I decided to take the inside line. I imagined I would get round the top of the lake quite quickly, but I'm afraid it took even longer, and was far harder than swimming in a straight line!

Eventually, I made it onto the straight, now aiming down the lake. This was the lido side, so it felt like familiar territory. The lido itself was roughly opposite the start and finish line, and the thought of getting a nice whiff of bacon cooking made me go a little bit faster. Unfortunately, the only thing I could smell was something that smelled a lot like sewage, so I shut down any thoughts of smelling anything for the rest of the swim.

Halfway around that first lap, I went off course again, and this time I nearly swam into a kayak. It wasn't that bad, and I quickly recalibrated. Looking right down the lake, I found the purple buoy to aim for. With that in my sights, I made excellent progress and even began to notice some of the other swimmers. The pace was slow and for most of the time, you couldn't see a thing. It was so hard to gauge pace or progress in any way other than noticing where you were on the course and how long it seemed to be taking. I had even less clue about the latter because there was no time to examine the watch.

The lower end of the lake was easier to aim for than the top, because the Serpentine Bridge was just beyond the purple buoys, marking the end of the Serpentine and the start of the Long Water. It felt as though I'd made it around this bottom curve more efficiently than I had around the top. This lower bit of the lake seemed to have feathers all over the surface though, and I was glad that the rest of the lake hadn't been the same.

As I began to make my way back up the lake, I lined myself up with the yellow buoy at the halfway point, beside the start and finish line. So far, so good. However, when I started the second lap I had to muster the enthusiasm that had been fuelled by adrenaline at the start.

As if to test me, a small amount of water began to sneak into my right goggles. Then a bit more. Then it was leaking. I had to adjust it. Treading water, I fiddled around for a moment, trying to re-seal the goggles without trapping any lake water inside. A person in a kayak whizzed over to check on my welfare and, satisfied with my reply, whizzed off again. Finally, the goggles were sealed and off I swam.

Back at the top curve of the course, a new problem emerged. I needed to go to the loo. Well, I didn't have time for all that, I told myself and tried to ignore it. By the end of the curve, it became more pressing and impossible to ignore. I began to imagine what swimming three-quarters of a mile when desperate for the loo might feel like. You already know what I decided to do. And I wouldn't tell you about it except I think you need to know. I remembered instructor Val telling me I would have to "learn to pee in my wetsuit", by which I'd assumed she had meant simply accepting the notion, rather than learning how to do it. It turns out, that peeing in a lake with a wetsuit on isn't the straightforward process we're used to. To my annoyance, when I decided to just go, nothing happened! I had to force it! At the same time, it dawned on me how many other people must be doing the same. I felt a wave of nausea wash over me and resolved yet again not to ingest a single drop of the lake.

By the time I reached the lido again - the halfway point of the second lap or 1.5 miles, I had recovered and was powering along with new vigour, and I think I had mastered it. There was only half a mile to go and I had plenty of energy left. I'd also mastered the buoy arrangement, and I was sighting – or was it spotting? – flawlessly, too.

Making the turn into the final curve, for the last time was a breeze. I tried to accelerate, but I'm not sure it made much difference. Some ducks made their way over to me for the second half of the final curve but bobbed off after a moment.

Only a quarter of a mile to go! I told myself to concentrate on the matter at hand and then realised I needed to find the finish line. Vaguely aware of the fact that swimmers were wearing different coloured hats according to their start wave, I glanced around as much as I could, looking for someone – anyone – wearing a blue hat, so that I might be able to follow them to the line. There must have been someone, but I couldn't identify a single person. All the hats looked the same; dark and shiny.

On I went, still trying to work out the apparent complexities of the finishing layout ahead. Logic told me to stick to the left since when I had passed the start and finish line the last time, I had stuck to the right. Damn! Why hadn't I cased the joint on my way past?! Suddenly, a manned kayak appeared alongside me again. "Everything OK?" "NO!" I yelled. "I need to find the finish line." "Stick to the left," he instructed. "How far to the left?" I asked, "I don't want to go round again!" I felt almost as confident as he sounded that I wouldn't miss the finish line, but I certainly wanted to make sure. Although not exactly tired, I was beginning to feel impatient for the finish.

I ploughed on for another few hundred metres before looking again. Sure enough, the finish line was in sight and I was aiming straight for it! There was no way of going off course and there were a few exit ramps to choose from. I aimed for the one furthest to the left, because I was already lined up with it.

This final few hundred metres went by more quickly than any of the other parts of the swim. The next time I looked up, the finishing line was in front of me. There were rails on each side of the ramp. They were too far apart to hold onto both, but I managed it anyway. Arms stretched out, I tucked my knees up to my chest, planted my feet on the ramp and catapulted myself up onto the floating walkway. To my surprise, my legs immediately worked without a fuss.

There were very few people around. I looked for James and Marmite and listened carefully for my mother, who'd said she planned to come and whose voice is unmistakable.

I followed what looked like the path to the medals – it was. But only the medal for the swim.

I borrowed a phone from someone incredibly kind and tapped in my mother's number – it's been the same since I was 14. It turned out that they were at the finish line and I had missed them, so I retraced my steps.

Mum gave me some water and James gave me the wristband. We all plodded back down to collect my London Classics medal – it was magnificent and satisfyingly heavy! The poor cycling medal would seem even more pitiful by comparison. The medal for the swim itself was pretty good too, and I'd barely given it any attention. The two medals clanked against each other, as, listening to stories about James' recent trip to Mongolia, we walked to the kiosk to buy sandwiches. Back under the trees, I dried off, shared my sandwiches with Marmite and opened the birthday presents my mother had brought, despite it being a day early. Mission accomplished!

The End

HARRIET GOULD

Afterthoughts

As you probably gathered, I had considered learning to swim a necessary evil, because I wanted to do the London Classics challenge to get the medal. A perfectly worthy though slightly pointless motivation. And although I'm very pleased to have the medal, I gained so much more from learning to swim than I ever dreamed possible.

You might have thought that I would have gained something from running a marathon or from cycling 100 miles as well, but learning to swim was the star of the show.

I probably took three things in total from the experience. If the medal was one of them, these are the other two.

I developed a new fearlessness of... well... everything!

Before I learned to swim, I was scared of most things. Scared of trying, scared of making mistakes. Scared of getting things wrong. I would assume I couldn't do anything, my default was "I can't". I'm sure there must be a reason, but let's not worry about that. Since learning to swim, things have changed. The world now appears to me as a playground, glittering with opportunity. It always was in a way, only, it seemed as though it was a playground for other people and not for me. Now I can swim, I've realised it's my playground too.

The third thing I've gained from the experience is swimming itself. I had assumed that after the event, just as I hadn't cycled since the race, I would never swim again. Not so. Powering through the water, completely submerged, is an other-worldly experience of which I have yet to tire. You breathe deliberately and the bubbles rush past your ears. It cleanses the mind in the way that I imagine a month in a meditation retreat might.

Now I can swim, I do it everywhere I can. Two days after the Serpentine swim, I went to Dubai for a conference and swam twice every day. First thing in the morning and last thing at night. And a few weeks after that, I was enjoying an ice-cold rooftop pool in Barcelona.

Before the event, I just wouldn't have dreamed of swimming on a work trip. Now I can't imagine not swimming.

It's tempting to wish I had learned sooner, but I think perhaps it happened at the right time.

The Other End

Kit List

As promised, here is a short glossary of the items I used along the way.

For the swimming...

Swimming costumes

ROXY, Speedo endurance and ARENA. In that order.

The ARENA costume has less material and I found it much better for energetic swimming.

Wetsuit, O'Neill 'shortie'

Goggles and other face kit

Speedo and Slazenger.

The main goggles were Speedo after I'd left the Slazenger ones behind one day.

Nose clip and earplugs also Slazenger.

I never wore earplugs in the end, but if I swim in very cold water again, I will.

Hats

Speedo for long hair from Amazon.

Plus the ones gifted by the two instructors and the ones I wore for the event that I received as part of the "race pack", along with the timing tag, wristbands etc.

Towels

Good Hair Day for curly hair.

Any other towels are fine.

Flipflops

Not completely necessary but generally the done thing. Use whatever you have. I did.

Watches

Garmin Swim2 is supposedly the best for swimming.

It worked well in the pool, but out of the measurable lake swims I used it for, it measured only one.

For the cycling...

Bike

TREK AL2, blue.

It was measured for me, and I was reassured that it was up to the task.

It turns out that the more the bike costs, the less likely it is that pedals are included.

I bought some very basic pedals to be going on with.

Footwear

Pedals, cleats, shoes (Specialized brand) and a pair of socks all came from Rutland Cycle. I took the bike back to Evans to get the pedals fitted.

I attached the cleats to the shoes at home.

Shorts

Padded bib shorts from Peloton De Paris.

These shorts were excellent. I didn't know they were on for the whole day (apart from the infamous loo stop).

Layers

Rapha vest as a wicking layer which I bought from someone on eBay

Evans jersey which had three big pockets across the back and a zip neck.

Hat

Peak-less ABUS hat, which meant I could see in front of me with my head down.

I did already have a hat, but it was heavy, and the peak restricted my line of vision so one week before the ride I ordered the new one. Fortunately, it fit. It turned out to be much lighter too.

Sunglasses

Gobi Cycle

Normal sunglasses didn't work with the hat, so I had to get cycling-specific ones. Adverts began to appear on Instagram, so I went with it and, luckily, they were a perfect fit.

Gloves

TK Maxx.

I wore fingerless, lightly padded gloves. They were the only thing I already had that I could use for the ride. I think they're meant for weightlifting (which I don't do).

Watch

Garmin Swim2. It worked better for the one-hundred-mile bike ride than it did for the two-mile lake swim.

Bike accessories

TOPEAK pouch strapped under the back of the seat.

Amazon and Evans bottle holders.

Camelbak water bottles.

Garmin Speedometer on loan from Jules and Joolz.

Shopper bike lock, vintage, belonging to Grandma Diana.

And for the sake of completeness, the kit list for running:

Footwear

Trainers, Asics GT 2000, practically by prescription after a gait test. I snapped my ankle years ago, so good heel support was essential.

Socks, Decathlon.

Clothes

Vest and bra from Sweaty Betty.

Nike shorts up to about 10k.

Ronhill shorts for running further than 10k. They had several pockets and more breathable material.

Sunglasses

Goodr. My first and only running-specific sunglasses. They're weightless and non-slip.

Hat

Buff lightweight baseball cap I had to train in the summer and this saved me from getting sunstroke.

Watch

Garmin VevoActive 3 was my watch at the time...

The Final End

HARRIET GOULD

About the Author

Harriet Gould was born in London and represented Great Britain on the junior show jumping squad before forging a career in advertising, initially working with brands including National Boat Shows, Crufts and Taste of London. Now specialising in the science and technology sector, Harriet hosts the weekly podcast "Lab Matters."

HARRIET GOULD

About PublishU

PublishU is transforming the world of publishing.

PublishU has developed a new and unique approach to publishing books, offering a three-step guided journey to becoming a globally published author!

We enable hundreds of people a year to write their book within 100-days, publish their book in 100-days and launch their book over 100-days to impact tens of thousands of people worldwide.

The journey is transformative, one author said,

"I never thought I would be able to write a book, let alone in 100 days... now I'm asking myself what else have I told myself that can't be done that actually can?'"

To find out more visit
www.PublishU.com

HARRIET GOULD

Printed in Great Britain
by Amazon